Black Ballerinas

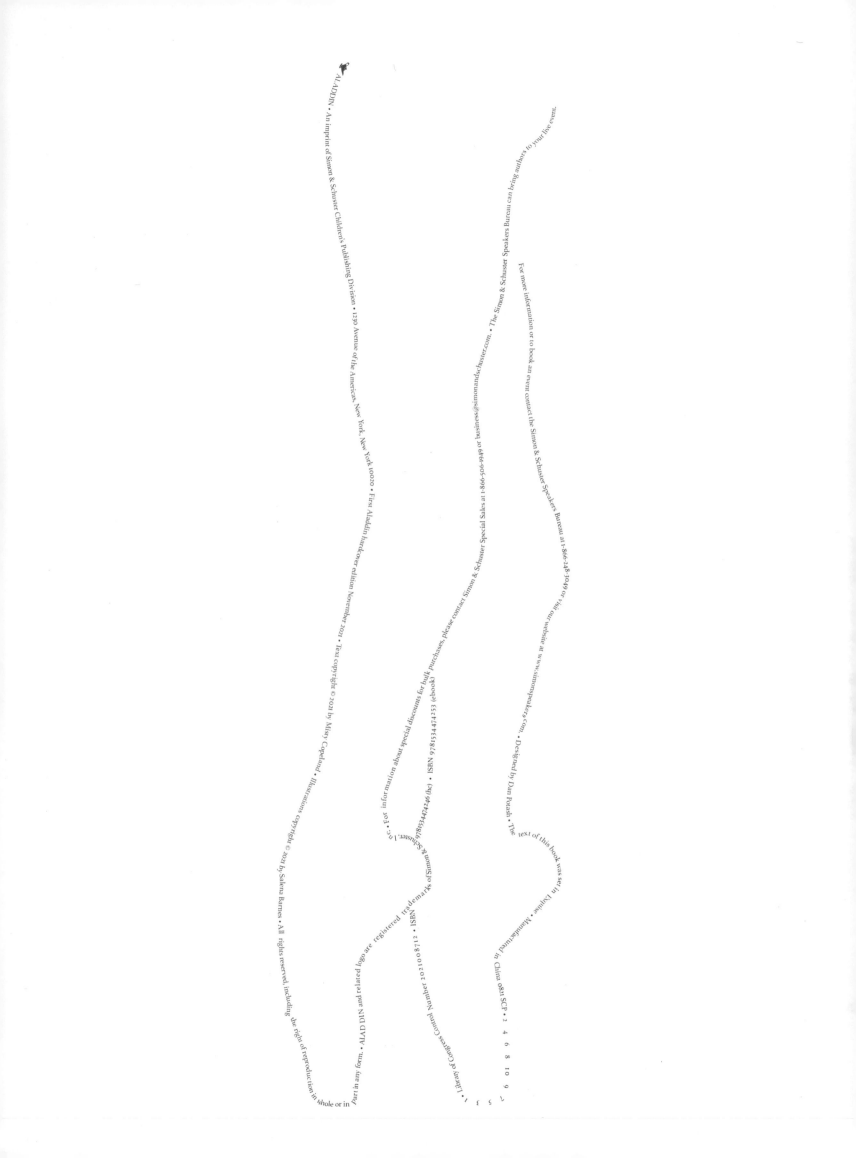

ALADDIN • An imprint of Simon & Schuster Children's Publishing Division • 1230 Avenue of the Americas, New York, New York 10020 • First Aladdin hardcover edition November 2021 • Text copyright © 2021 by Misty Copeland • Illustrations copyright © 2021 by Salena Barnes • All rights reserved, including the right of reproduction in whole or in Part in any form. • ALADDIN and related logo are registered trademarks of Simon & Schuster, Inc. • For information about special discounts for bulk purchases, please contact Simon & Schuster Special Sales at 1-866-506-1949 or business@simonandschuster.com. • The Simon & Schuster Speakers Bureau can bring authors to your live event. For more information or to book an event contact the Simon & Schuster Speakers Bureau at 1-866-248-3049 or visit our website at www.simonspeakers.com. • Designed by Dan Potash • The text of this book was set in Expirise. Manufactured in China 0821 SCP • 2 4 6 8 10 9 7 5 3 1 • Library of Congress Control Number 2021001712 • ISBN 9781534474246 (hc) • ISBN 9781534474253 (ebook)

Black Ballerinas
My Journey to Our Legacy

MISTY COPELAND

ILLUSTRATED BY **SALENA BARNES**

ALADDIN
NEW YORK LONDON TORONTO SYDNEY NEW DELHI

This is for anyone who has searched to find his or her reflection.
For our forebears, who laid the foundation but could only dream of our accomplishments.
And for the future of ballet, in hopes that it will continue striving to be better,
to see us, to hear us, and to celebrate us.
—M. C.

For my parents, my brother, and all Black and brown children,
to encourage them to believe in their dreams and make them come true.
—S. B.

With special thanks to Michelle Meadows for her contributions.

*L*ike many young women growing up, I struggled to find my place and voice in the world, but "Black" was the one label I confidently wore with pride—it was one of the only things that was tangible and made sense in my very chaotic young life.

This was true until I discovered ballet at the age of thirteen. Ballet would provide a natural and strong identity for me, and throughout high school, I was simply known as "the ballerina."

I entered the ballet world and was completely immersed in the beauty, blinded by my love and passion, and protected by my teachers, who created a bubble for me to exist in to focus solely on my training. It was a shock to my system when I joined American Ballet Theatre (ABT) four years later and I was no longer being shielded from the reality that I was a Black girl in a very white ballet world.

When I became a professional ballet dancer with ABT twenty years ago, my journey of true self-identity began. I spent the first decade of my career alone, the only Black woman in a company of eighty-plus dancers. I struggled to find my voice and define who I was in this space. I attempted to find others like me. I dug, I read, and I researched, uncovering so many of the Black ballerinas who came before me—dancers whose stories have not been told in earnest. So many of these women helped me to understand myself and discover my history.

Part of my mission is to bring awareness to the contributions of Black ballerinas. To give a sense of the rich histories of those who may not be documented in ballet history books, yet whose careers—and legacies—are no less valuable and inspiring.

This is in no way a comprehensive list of Black ballerinas; this is a list that is personal to my journey and hopefully a starting point for others to begin to do their own research. When discussing Black and brown ballerinas, I would be remiss if I didn't acknowledge and highlight the real issue of colorism both inside and outside the Black community and how it has impacted what is presented onstage. There are varying forms of privilege in the world. I acknowledge that being biracial and/or lighter skinned is a privilege both in the world and in ballet. This privilege does not extend just to me but has dictated access and opportunity throughout our history, and so often not equitably. Black dancers are not a monolith, but it is my hope that the success of any of us will ultimately allow for the success of all of us.

In this book, I'm going to share my personal stories about, connections to, and experiences with these groundbreaking women.

Here are intimate snapshots of my discovery of and relationships to these women. I am infinitely grateful for their legacies. This is my bow to these amazing dancers.

Misty Copeland

"What's wonderful about being a ballerina is being able to tell a story without saying a single word."

Lauren Anderson

(born 1965)

I can draw a direct line from Lauren Anderson to my own existence as a Black ballerina. I was seventeen years old the first time I saw Lauren, when she graced the cover of *Dance Magazine* in 1999. I was stopped dead in my tracks. Her dark-hued skin illuminated the page and filled me with immense pride. I think the impact of her image on me was more than I could comprehend at the time. Because of mainstream standards of beauty, and the weight associated with being a dark-skinned woman in our society, it was an anomaly to see her beauty in all its glory representing the very white and exclusive ballet world.

With all the excitement I felt, at the same time it hit me that I had been missing an important piece of classical ballet history. As a pre-professional ballet student, I had never before seen a Black ballerina on the cover of a dance publication—and it would change everything for me.

Lauren has been a mentor and friend of mine since we met while American Ballet Theatre (ABT) was touring through Texas in 2006, the same year Lauren retired from the stage. With all of the beautiful experiences we've shared over the years, the most incredible was in June 2015, when Lauren presented me with flowers during my bows at the Metropolitan Opera House after my New York City debut as the lead in *Swan Lake*. I was overwhelmed with love, support, and the significance of that historical moment. Lauren was the first Black ballerina to dance the lead in *Swan Lake* with the Houston Ballet, and that moment on the Met stage was a passing of the torch to me, the first Black ballerina to dance the lead in *Swan Lake* with ABT.

Lauren's journey in the ballet world began at the Houston Ballet Academy. When her mother took her to see Dance Theatre of Harlem, Lauren was inspired by the first Black ballerina she ever saw perform: Virginia Johnson.

Another turning point in her life occurred when Ben Stevenson, Lauren's mentor, and then artistic director of the Houston Ballet, cast her in the lead role in *Alice's Adventures in Wonderland*. When Lauren asked him why she had been chosen for a role that had traditionally gone to white ballerinas, he answered, "Darling, you're a dancer and dancers dance. The only color in art is on a canvas."

Lauren danced with the Houston Ballet from 1983 to 2006. In 1990 Lauren became the first African American to be promoted to principal dancer at the Houston Ballet. But her groundbreaking success wasn't universally accepted. Lauren found out years later that her company had shielded her as much as possible from racist remarks, hate mail, and even death threats.

And in her current role as program manager in the Houston Ballet's Education and Community Engagement program, she is helping create more firsts, like our respective *Swan Lake* performances, because she knows how critical they are for sparking change.

Lauren's perseverance and success have profoundly impacted me. I believe it is so important to support one another as we embark on our individual journeys, because we are all working to create a brighter future for the next generation, and Lauren has done and continues to do that in a multitude of ways.

"The saying 'Never forget where you came from' was something that was taught to me as a very young girl, and I carry these words like a badge of honor."

Aesha Ash

(born 1977)

I became aware of Aesha Ash in 2000, my senior year of high school. She was the dancing double for actress Zoe Saldana in the hit movie *Center Stage*. Five years my senior and dancing for New York City Ballet (NYCB), she was the epitome of beauty, grace, and strength in my eyes. Not until Aesha left NYCB after eight years with the company would I learn of all her struggles as a Black ballerina—struggles that I would also face in my own career.

We were each the only Black woman in our respective ballet companies for a significant number of years. The weight of this reality, along with the lack of support and understanding that often comes with being the "only," left space for doubt to creep in. Microaggressions, like coded language about our Black bodies being a distraction onstage and not having the right shades of makeup available, were never hard to decipher. Nor did their subtlety make them hurt any less. These veiled comments and slights can easily chip away at one's identity and self-worth, a common experience among Black ballerinas. After leaving NYCB in 2003, Aesha joined Béjart Ballet Lausanne in Switzerland as a soloist. Two years later she joined Alonzo King LINES Ballet in San Francisco, and then toured with Morphoses/The Wheeldon Company between 2007 and 2008.

Eventually all of the traumas Aesha endured over the years about her race took their toll, pushing her to almost say goodbye to the dance world altogether. However, Aesha crafted a second act for herself in which she was able to approach dance on her own terms. In 2011 she channeled her experiences into creating the Swan Dreams Project, using ballet and photography as a way to combat stereotypes and the objectification of Black women in ballet.

Growing up in Rochester, New York, Aesha hadn't seen Black ballerinas. She remembers how she felt when, after starting at NYCB's School of American Ballet (SAB), she saw a photo of ballerina Andrea Long-Naidu, who danced with NYCB and Dance Theatre of Harlem. Seeing the photo of a successful Black ballerina gave her hope, and through the Swan Dreams Project, she wants to make sure aspiring dancers of color know they belong in these spaces too.

Aesha, with a performer's resilience and stamina, had another trick up her sleeve for her third act. When George Balanchine founded NYCB in 1948, he implemented a system that relied on students from the school and dancers from the company to eventually return as teachers and staff; however, this opportunity was rarely extended to its few Black alumni.

Over six decades later, in a full-circle move back to her old stomping grounds of NYCB, Aesha made history when she became the first Black female member of SAB's permanent faculty in their eighty-six-year history. The opportunity for her not only to pass on her immense knowledge and experiences to the next generation of dancers but also to serve as a role model and mentor to Black and brown ballerinas is a huge deal and a step in the right direction for inclusion and representation in ballet.

"I knew when I was ten years old that this is where I want to be, this is where I want to go, and this is my dream."

Debra **Austin**

(born 1955)

In 1982, the same year that I was born, Debra Austin rose to prominence as the first Black woman to be promoted to principal ballerina with the Pennsylvania Ballet. After I joined American Ballet Theatre, I began to understand the difficulties of being a Black woman in a ballet company with predominantly white dancers, but it would be some time before I learned about Debra's experience of being the first and could more intimately relate to both her struggles and triumphs.

Debra's first ballet teacher told her parents she had no talent. She was nine years old, and the negative feedback led her parents to seek ballet lessons elsewhere. They took her to Christine Neubert's Children's Ballet Theatre in New York, where she was taught by Barbara Walczak, a former soloist with New York City Ballet (NYCB). Seeing Debra's gift for dance, Barbara connected Debra with Diana Adams, then director of the School of American Ballet (SAB). Debra joined SAB at age twelve—with a full Ford Foundation scholarship.

While this was huge for Debra and her dancing career, someone recognizing your talent and potential doesn't necessarily change the obstacle of race in ballet. At fourteen, she was told NYCB was out of her reach because she wouldn't blend into the corps de ballet for *Swan Lake*. This awful "blending" euphemism and other coded language are used to communicate that our Black and brown bodies don't belong in classical ballets. And, sadly, it's something that Black and brown ballerinas are still dealing with today.

But instead of giving up, Debra pressed on. And George Balanchine—influential choreographer and cofounder of NYCB—took notice of Debra when he saw her dance in class. In 1971, sixteen-year-old Debra was invited to join the company by Balanchine himself, making her the first African American woman hired into NYCB. There Debra danced numerous principal roles, including in *Ballo della Regina*, for which Balanchine created a solo for her. After nine years with NYCB, Debra went on to dance principal roles with the Zurich Ballet in Switzerland and toured throughout Europe.

When Debra returned to the States, she made history as the first Black principal female dancer at the Pennsylvania Ballet. But even in her new position, Debra still encountered people who doubted her.

After she was cast as the Sylph in *La Sylphide*, someone staging the ballet questioned the decision, stating that she had never seen a Black Sylph. Given that a sylph is a mythological fairylike creature, the artistic director challenged the stager and replied, "Have you ever seen a sylph before?"

Debra stared doubt right in the eyes and said, "I deserve to be here." She faced historical barricades with the courage to be the first, carving out a trailblazing career that set the bar for us all.

"You fall in love with it. Your body falls in love with it."

Joan Myers Brown

(born 1931)

One of the most common excuses I have heard throughout my career as to why there is such a lack of diversity in ballet is that schools and companies don't know where to find dancers of color. Joan Myers Brown took matters into her own hands and addressed that "problem" head-on.

Too often when people speak of diversity in ballet, they are just focused on the stage. So much of my strength and will to be my best has come from a sense of support I've felt by seeing representation all around me. We need more Black and brown dancers on the stage, but we also need more Black and brown teachers, stagehands, costumers, and makeup artists in major ballet companies. This would go a long way toward creating a supportive and sensitive environment for dancers of color. And Joan did just that, creating and building a dance organization that has trained and nurtured generations of Black and brown dancers.

Joan discovered ballet in high school, but racial discrimination kept her from being able to join ballet classes. She sought the Black ballet teachers giving Black children opportunities to learn ballet, going on to study with Essie Marie Dorsey, and then later with Marion Cuyjet and Sydney King. Marion Cuyjet became a huge influence on Joan, with the two forming a relationship that would span decades.

Joan also studied with Antony Tudor, who taught at the Philadelphia Ballet Guild. A dancer and choreographer, he became an ally for Black dancers during that time. When the students learned *The Sleeping Beauty*, the white dancers refused to partner Joan. Mr. Tudor partnered her himself. The example he set for Joan motivated her to go on to provide training for Black dancers.

Because opportunities for Black ballerinas to dance in ballet companies were limited, Joan was eventually forced to pivot. She danced in nightclub tours for several years—en pointe and in heels—where she was often the only Black dancer in the show.

Eventually, Joan returned to Philadelphia, determined to give young people the same opportunities she had not been given. In 1960 she founded the Philadelphia School of Dance Arts. As Joan grew her school, her former teacher Marion Cuyjet became a mentor and teacher to her in a new way.

But when Joan's students got older, they couldn't find work with dance companies in Philadelphia. So Joan helped found the Philadelphia Dance Company, PHILADANCO, in 1970 so those aspiring dancers wouldn't have to abandon their dreams of becoming professional ballet dancers. In 1988 she helped form the International Association of Blacks in Dance to address the lack of opportunities, funding, and touring for Black dance companies. It's empowering to see my community create opportunities for itself. Because of Joan, we have hope, giving the Black community a space to thrive and the broader dance world the platform to find us.

Joan's passion is creating opportunity for Black children because of her own experience of having other Black women generate support and opportunity for her. Joan is a Philly legend, not just for her dancing but for her unbelievable leadership and for carrying on the teachings of two icons—Sydney King and Marion Cuyjet.

"One of the things that I loved very much was learning a language."

Delores Browne

(born 1935)

Delores Browne's passion for ballet is what really drew me to her and her journey. In Delores, I found a kindred "bunhead" spirit. With a love of all things ballet and a natural affinity for performing, we were one and the same.

Delores's mental strength, discipline, and dedication were all traits I recognized in myself. While ballet has not always been welcoming to Black and brown dancers, I've also heard the falsehood that we, as Black people, have made the choice not to engage with it. In contrast, Delores showed me that it was okay for a brown girl to have an enthusiastic devotion to this art form.

That devotion started for Delores at a young age. She was a big fan of actress and dancer Cyd Charisse, and seeing Cyd dance en pointe inspired Delores to want to do the same. But when she tried to enroll in ballet classes in Philadelphia, she was always put on a waiting list. Her mother shielded Delores from knowing that she was not getting into schools because of racial discrimination.

Eventually, Delores joined the ballet club in school, and at fourteen, she was offered a scholarship to the Judimar School, run by former dancer Marion Cuyjet. Marion, a fair-skinned Black woman, dreamed of producing the first Black American ballerina. She recognized Delores's gift for dance, and Delores quickly became the star ballerina of Judimar.

One summer, Marion registered Delores and other students for classes at Ballet Arts at Carnegie Hall. But when she went to sign in, Delores was told there must have been a mistake, and she was declined admission. Delores stood up for herself and insisted that she either get to take the class or get her money back. She was eventually admitted, and Delores became one of the first Black dancers to ever study at Ballet Arts.

At seventeen, Delores successfully auditioned for the New York City Ballet's School of American Ballet (SAB) as one of only a few students of color. Quickly realizing she would likely never be asked to join the company, Delores left SAB after only one year.

Back home, Delores finally got her big break when she was offered a contract with Ballet Americana, a company of Black dancers. It was the opportunity of a lifetime. When they went on tour in Europe, they were renamed the New York Negro Ballet, because the tour's promoter wanted audiences to know it was a Black company. As a soloist and principal dancer, Delores danced in the Bluebird pas de deux in *The Sleeping Beauty* and performed in other ballets on tour.

After the ballet company's patron passed unexpectedly and the original company dissolved, companies back home would not hire Delores. Discouraged, she stopped dancing. But one phone call brought Delores back. John Jones, whom she had partnered with previously, was curating a concert for the Lincoln Center library theater and invited her to perform with him as his partner. After years of trying to prove herself to the institution of ballet, it was her Philadelphia family and the Black ballet community that gave her an amazing second act. After the concert, the offers flooded in, and she went on to perform with the Alicia Alonso Ballet Company. Delores eventually became director of the Ailey School's scholarship program in the 1970s, and taught classes there and at Joan Myers Brown's PHILADANCO.

Although Delores didn't get to have the career she deserved because of the color of her skin, her passion for both ballet and her community has opened doors and laid the foundation for me and so many others to thrive. She is a voice for change in ballet through her teaching, commitment, and love for giving back. Every part of Delores's journey has made it that much easier for me to become a principal dancer. She is an American ballet pioneer!

"Both art and dance were the two great loves of my life."

Janet Collins

(1917–2003)

One evening in the summer of 2013, I was preparing to make my debut as the Queen of the Dryads in *Don Quixote* at the Metropolitan Opera House. As I worked to calm and focus my mind before the show, I caught a reflection of myself in the mirror and was struck by the familiarity of what I saw. In that moment I saw how my own image was an almost identical copy of a photo of Janet Collins in her dressing room at the Met decades earlier—from our skin tones to the shape of our foreheads and the tight buns on top of our heads, and even the bouquets of flowers surrounding us in our dressing rooms.

By this time I had already begun my personal mission to research the Black ballerinas who had come before me, and Janet was one of the first on my list. As the first Black ballerina to perform with the Metropolitan Opera on the Met stage, she had entered one of the most exclusive clubs that any dancer, let alone a Black woman, could join. I have an overwhelming sense of pride that I'm now part of that group. In that brief moment, before the biggest debut in my life up to that point, Janet Collins reminded me that I belonged.

Joining the classical ballet world was no easy feat for Janet. As a little girl, she wanted to study at one of the more prominent ballet schools in Los Angeles, but she was turned away because of her race. Despite this setback, Janet persevered, eventually taking private lessons. As a teenager in the 1930s, she auditioned for the Ballet Russe de Monte Carlo. However, racial segregation in the South kept Black dancers from sharing the stage with white dancers on tour. The director said if he hired her, she would have to paint her skin white to blend in with the other dancers onstage, disguising the fact that she was Black. But Janet declined.

After this heartbreaking setback, Janet, like many other Black and brown dancers, was forced to pivot into theatrical dancing, where she thrived. She won a Donaldson Award for her performance on Broadway in the production of Cole Porter's musical *Out of This World*.

After her win, Janet made history when she became the first Black principal ballerina hired by the Met on November 13, 1951. She performed at the Met until 1954, dancing lead roles in operas such as *Aida* and *Carmen*. After she left the Met, she went on tour, choreographed shows, and taught dance at several institutions, inspiring a new generation of dancers.

Our debuts at the Met being separated by over sixty years makes me think about the progress made in ballet since Janet's debut as well as how much further we still have to go. Even now, Black and brown ballerinas are being asked to try to "blend" in with their mainly white colleagues—something I myself have been asked to do in the past.

I dance in honor of trailblazers like Janet who faced the ugliness of racism head-on, who were asked to deny who they were just to continue dancing.

Janet opened the door so that many more Black and brown ballerinas like me might also have the opportunity to see their faces in a Metropolitan Opera House dressing room mirror.

"*It was so exciting. As soon as it was discovered that there were Black kids dancing in the Russian style, I was in the limelight.*"

Marion Cuyjet

(1920–1996)

Marion Cuyjet's story is the definition of what it means to bring your people with you. She was a natural leader with a passion for creating a better future for the next generation. I've found that this form of leadership and the desire to share one's knowledge and experience are common to ballerinas and Black women alike. Perhaps it is because of the necessity for the tradition and wisdom in Black culture and in the ballet community to be passed down by the "doers."

Marion provided me with the blueprint for how I want to use my voice and platform. I have always understood the impact of representation, but learning of her contributions to the Black ballet community has allowed me to see even more clearly the impact that one committed person can have on the whole. She showed me the importance of being more than just an image on the stage—the power of being a real person in the community, someone others can see, touch, and feel. In this way, she taught so many dancers who would go on to teach even more dancers, like Judith Jamison, Delores Browne, and Joan Myers Brown, creating a path for generations of Black ballerinas to change the world.

Marion began her ballet training in Philadelphia in the 1930s with Essie Marie Dorsey, a pioneer in her own right. Like Marion, Essie was fair-skinned, which could be useful to work around racial barriers. Essie became Marion's mentor and helped her gain admission to the Littlefield Ballet school (which later became the Philadelphia Ballet) even though Black students were not admitted. With West African, British, and Native American ancestry, Marion had a fair complexion. Though her family chose not to pass, the school's directors didn't know Marion was Black until some of her Black friends came to see her after a performance. In response, Marion was asked to leave the school and not come back. Essie helped arrange for Marion to receive private lessons. In 1946, Marion partnered with Sydney King, another former student of Essie's, to open the Sydney-Marion School of Dance. The two parted ways a couple of years later, and Marion launched the Judimar School of Dance.

Though Marion did not dance professionally, she found a bigger purpose in teaching and was fearless in pushing boundaries. Marion was the first Black woman to rent space in downtown Philadelphia, before being evicted when people realized she had Black students. She had to move her studio several times due to racism, but despite this, her students always followed her. Regardless of the many barriers they faced, Marion was dedicated to expanding her students' horizons, taking them on trips to study at New York ballet studios. When she opened Judimar, Marion's dream was to produce the first Black American ballerina—a vision that was the driving force behind her demanding so much of her students. Marion was a pioneer who devoted her life to giving Black students opportunities at a time when ballet schools in Philadelphia would not accept them, using her ability to pass in what were mainly white spaces—to her students' advantage. She sent the elevator back down time and time again, as her mentor Essie had done for her.

Marion is a part of a lineage that helped to develop and empower an incredible number of Black dancers, a legacy she has inspired me to continue through mentorship and advocacy.

"I don't just want to be a ballerina playing the role. I want to be out there being that flashy, superstrong woman."

Stephanie **Dabney**

(born 1958)

In 1982, two Firebirds were born. While I would not dance the role for three decades, in 1982, Stephanie Dabney became the first African American ballerina to perform the title role of Firebird in Dance Theatre of Harlem's (DTH's) production.

In 2012, thirty years after Stephanie's debut as the Firebird, I was in the DTH studios working on a project with the company on the day I learned that I was cast as the Firebird in American Ballet Theatre's (ABT's) production. It was a beautifully serendipitous moment, being surrounded by a group of Black ballet dancers who understood my journey.

As I thought about how best to approach the iconic Firebird role, and what it would mean for me as the first Black woman to perform the role with ABT, I hoped to embody the warmth, fire, and passion of Stephanie's spirit—she had made the role her own, so much so that it became her legacy.

As a young child, Stephanie was enrolled in dance classes at Ballet Western Reserve in Youngstown, Ohio. When the Alvin Ailey American Dance Theater came to town, it was the first time she saw professional dancers who looked like her, and the sight of Black dancers gave her hope that she too could have a professional career in dance.

But as she progressed, and despite her obvious talents, roles in recitals were not offered to her. That all changed the following summer when DTH came to Youngstown. Stephanie enrolled in a DTH class led by founder and artistic director Arthur Mitchell, who had become the first African American principal dancer at New York City Ballet in 1962. Mr. Mitchell invited Stephanie to join DTH as an apprentice in 1975. She eventually became a principal dancer, performing with DTH through the mid-1990s as part of the new guard of celebrated Black ballerinas that Mr. Mitchell was nurturing at DTH.

Though her repertoire was impressive, it was the Firebird role that became her signature: fiery, passionate, and strong. In large part due to Stephanie's beautiful interpretation of the role, and with elaborate costumes and sets designed by the late artistic visionary Geoffrey Holder, *Firebird* became one of DTH's most beloved and recognized ballets.

Stephanie went on to perform as the Firebird around the world, including at the opening ceremonies of the 1984 Olympics.

In 2015, having never met her, I was honored to have Stephanie at my debut as Odette/Odile in *Swan Lake* with ABT. I remember after the performance, in the lobby of the Metropolitan Opera House, with a flurry of well-wishers surrounding me, a calm settled over me when I locked eyes with Stephanie. The two of us wrapped each other up in the warmest embrace—fittingly, in front of the displayed costume I had worn in my own Firebird debut three years earlier.

Although she had long ago hung up her brown pointe shoes, she understood exactly what my performance had meant, and we shared in the celebration of the legacies of Black ballerinas, including herself, who had fought and persevered, eventually making my career possible. It felt as if Stephanie had passed the torch to me so I could help carry her legacy—and the Firebird—forward to new generations soon to discover the beauty of ballet.

"All I knew is that I wanted to be a ballerina."

Frances Taylor Davis

(1920–2018)

I have been incredibly fortunate to have collected the A-team of mentors throughout my life. Frances Taylor Davis was one of them. Not only was she an incredible wealth of knowledge, experience, and stories, but she also gave me a sense of my purpose and history, and became one of the driving forces behind my desire to write this book.

Frances experienced an unbelievably full and diverse performing career, but her classical accomplishments have gone unnoticed and, to some extent, have nearly been erased. She started taking ballet when she was eight and was en pointe by age ten. Frances studied with Mildred Hessler, who helped her get into the Edna McRae School of Dance in Chicago, and she became the only Black student enrolled there when she arrived. At just sixteen, Frances performed the role of the Swan Queen in *Swan Lake* and the Sugar Plum Fairy in *The Nutcracker*.

While on tour with the Katherine Dunham company in 1948, Frances was invited for a special presentation to dance with the Paris Opera Ballet, becoming the first African American to be invited to perform with the company. The fact that this milestone was not widely documented is a perfect example of erasure within the Black ballet community and of why I feel such a responsibility to tell these stories.

Frances later appeared with Sammy Davis Jr. in a production of *Porgy and Bess* and on Broadway in *Mr. Wonderful*, *Shinbone Alley*, and *West Side Story*. After marrying jazz icon Miles Davis, Frances reluctantly made the decision to leave the stage behind, but dance never left her heart.

Frances and I had numerous extensive phone conversations before meeting for the first time in 2014 at a gala hosted by another one of my mentors, Debbie Allen. That night, Frances told me incredible stories about her journey that I will never forget, including the one about her historic performance with the Paris Opera Ballet.

As Frances aged, I felt an urgency to hear everything she was willing to share with me, determined to help keep her legacy alive. Keenly aware that her accomplishments were not widely known, Frances encouraged me to research the Paris Opera Ballet in hopes of finding tangible evidence of her having performed with the company.

I stayed in touch with Frances during her final days, hoping to extend my time with her. Thankfully, her nephew knew of our relationship and how much her legacy and those of other Black dancers like his aunt meant to me, and he worked to keep us in contact.

The last words we shared were positive and beautiful. I let her know that my work was far from over and that I am forever grateful that I was welcomed into her life and heart. Frances longed for an artifact to memorialize her performance with the Paris Opera Ballet, and she held out hope that I could uncover a playbill from the show. And so, my mission continues.

"Turn your past, your scars, into your strength. That's what I always try to do."

Michaela DePrince

(born 1995)

Michaela DePrince is a one-of-a-kind dancer with a remarkable journey. Originally named Mabinty Bangura, she was born during Sierra Leone's civil war. After losing both parents, she was placed in an orphanage before being adopted by the DePrince family and moving to New Jersey. Beyond her great talent, it is Michaela's perseverance and ambition that I truly admire.

Michaela's love of ballet was inspired by a ballerina on a magazine cover she found as a child. Despite the support of her new family, Michaela's journey was not without some all too common obstacles. When Michaela was only eight years old, a teacher told her that she couldn't perform as Marie in *The Nutcracker* because America was not ready for a Black girl ballerina. Another teacher told her adoptive mother, who is white, that Black dancers weren't worth investing money in. Regardless, Michaela remained determined, stayed focused, and began making strides.

At fifteen, Michaela starred in the documentary film *First Position*, which followed six young dancers as they prepared for a prestigious ballet competition. Her win brought her to American Ballet Theatre's (ABT's) Jacqueline Kennedy Onassis (JKO) School, on scholarship, where I immediately took her under my wing. Michaela was a prodigious talent and the first darker-skinned dancer I witnessed come through the program. I knew she would need support. Colorism is, without a doubt, an issue in the professional ballet world. When companies and schools do accept Black women, the ballerinas tend to be biracial or light-skinned. And Michaela's vitiligo, a condition in which color is lost from areas of skin, further differentiates her aesthetic from most other dancers'.

As auditioning season ended, I was taken aback when Michaela's time at JKO did not result in an offer for a Studio Company contract. She was the brightest young star coming out of the school, and I was compelled to help her find her first professional opportunity in ballet. Time was of the essence. I asked one of my mentors, Dance Theatre of Harlem (DTH) artistic director Virginia Johnson, to take a look at this incredible talent. The union of dancer and company greatly benefited both, as DTH was preparing for its first season back on the stage after an eight-year hiatus. And at seventeen years old, Michaela joined as the youngest member in the company at the time.

Following her year with DTH, she traveled abroad to create the career she desired, joining the Dutch National Ballet's junior company in 2013 as the only Black dancer then. She rose through the ranks quickly with her promotion to the main company in 2014, and then to soloist in 2016.

Michaela's European move is reminiscent of so many Black ballerinas' journeys throughout history, as many went overseas in order to have the ballet careers they were denied in the US. It's sad that some things have remained the same in terms of ballet opportunities in America for women of color.

Michaela has had an incredible trajectory outside the ballet realm too. She collaborated with her mother to write her memoir, featured in Beyoncé's *Lemonade* visual album, will star in the film *Coppélia*, and has served as a brand spokesperson for several major companies. And since 2016 she has been an ambassador for War Child, a nonprofit organization that works to improve the well-being of children living with violence and armed conflict—providing resources that Michaela wished she could have had as a child.

The support I have received from Black and brown women has helped me achieve my success. Continuing this tradition, I have always felt a strong desire to help nurture and guide Michaela, and I make it a point to assure her that she has a sister and a support system in me. Michaela has earned every opportunity she's been given, and she is confidently carrying us into the future.

"If you have ballet, you can move forward in any direction in dance."

Nikisha Fogo

(born 1995)

It's pretty fitting that Nikisha Fogo's last name means "fire" in Portuguese, because she is truly a bright burning flame that has burst onto the ballet scene. In 2020, Nikisha made history when she became the first Black principal dancer with the San Francisco Ballet. But I became aware of her while she was still dancing with the Vienna State Ballet in Austria as a principal, and her expressive and powerfully layered dancing started flooding my social media feed. I remember feeling an overwhelming sense of pride learning about her, a biracial ballerina who was dancing leading roles in a classical company.

Getting to know Nikisha through our work together on a COVID-19 fundraising initiative, called Swans for Relief, has been both gratifying and inspiring. During a time of immense stress and uncertainty for both the world and the dance community, thirty-two ballerinas from across the globe joined forces to individually perform the iconic Dying Swan variation. Despite the mature sentimentality of the piece, Nikisha brought a full and vibrant intensity. The openness with which she gives of herself is what makes her such a unique artist.

Nikisha was born in Sweden, to a Swedish mother and British-born Jamaican father. They specialized in show dancing and hip-hop and opened one of the first hip-hop dance schools in Sweden. Music played all the time at home, and Nikisha and her sister shared their parents' love of dance.

Though Nikisha started training in hip-hop, tap, and jazz at a young age, every year, she watched ballerinas perform on television in the Vienna New Year's concert. At age nine she asked her parents if she could audition for the Royal Swedish Ballet School. She was accepted and has never looked back.

In 2011 she participated in the Prix de Lausanne, one of the world's most prestigious international ballet competitions. This resulted in multiple scholarship offers and opened the door to her future as a ballerina. Gailene Stock, then director of the Royal Ballet School in London, offered Nikisha the chance to train at the school, and she accepted.

Just two years later, Nikisha joined the Vienna State Ballet, rising quickly from the corps de ballet to demi-soloist in 2015, to soloist in 2016, and then to principal in 2018. Her promotion to principal was a surprise announcement at the curtain call of *Sylvia*—her first full-length principal role. She has since performed lead roles in *Coppélia*, *Don Quixote*, and numerous other ballets.

After an artistic leadership change at Vienna State Ballet, Nikisha decided it was time to seek other opportunities and found her new home at the San Francisco Ballet. Though she has only been there for a short time, she is already making an impact as the only Black principal dancer with the company.

Through my own experiences as a Black artist, I know that it can sometimes be difficult to be open and vulnerable when you don't feel safe or supported, particularly when you're not surrounded by people who look like you. Of course, as ballerinas, our goal is to make the nearly impossible appear effortless. Nikisha's dancing appears free and without inhibition or hesitation, seemingly unencumbered by the uniqueness of her position or the weight of history—giving me hope that times are changing.

"I have been able to continue and pass on
an art that was passed on to me."

Robyn **Gardenhire**

(born 1964)

Robyn Gardenhire etched a path that I would come to follow. I grew up in Los Angeles, California, like her, and went on to dance with American Ballet Theatre (ABT), also like her.

Robyn's own journey into ballet began as a young child. Her parents supported her love of dance, taking her to classes and auditions. One of those auditions was for the former Los Angeles Ballet's junior company, where she began to seriously train. Her talent was obvious, and she received scholarships to study at the ABT school, the New York City Ballet's School of American Ballet (SAB), and the San Francisco Ballet School.

At sixteen Robyn became the youngest Black dancer to be offered a contract with Joffrey II, the Joffrey Ballet's junior company. She then joined Cleveland Ballet, where she performed principal roles such as the Arabian Princess in *The Nutcracker* and the Russian Girl in *Serenade*.

Wanting to challenge herself artistically, Robyn toured all over Europe with Karole Armitage's modern dance company before returning to the United States.

Upon her return, Mikhail Baryshnikov personally invited her to dance with ABT and later with his White Oak Dance Project, a touring company he cofounded with Mark Morris.

Beyond her obvious talent and dance repertoire, what truly makes me feel connected to Robyn is the work she is doing in her community. Though she didn't see many Black ballerinas as she was growing up, Robyn believes that when children see people who look like them dancing onstage, it shows them they can do it too. She was the main force behind ABT's diversity committee and its Make a Ballet program, as well as a founding member of SAB's diversity committee.

Upon returning home to Los Angeles after her performing career came to a close, she created a dance institution: the City Ballet of Los Angeles (CBLA), which reflects the economic and racial diversity of that community. CBLA provides full scholarships, along with no-cost or low-cost classes, to students who are economically and socially disadvantaged. Robyn has said that without early scholarships, she wouldn't have been able to pursue her own career, and she knows how important these financial resources are for many aspiring ballerinas.

Through Robyn's candid interviews in my documentary, *A Ballerina's Tale*, she generously shared her experiences in an effort to help educate a broader audience on the difficulties and realities of existing as a Black ballerina in a very white world. Every Black ballerina who passed through ABT's doors made it that much more possible for me to go further.

I took my first ballet class in gym shorts and socks on the basketball court of a Boys & Girls Club. It takes visionaries like Robyn, and schools like CBLA, to give someone like me a chance to reach their full potential.

She is giving the next generation an opportunity to develop not only into ballerinas but into more fully developed young women. I am grateful to Robyn for making it possible for many girls to train and to dream, and I am humbled and inspired by her commitment to paying it forward.

"Treat every class as a performance, every coaching session as a performance-enhancing tool, and every performance as a way to capture the hearts of the audience."

Céline Gittens

(born 1988)

In 2012, as I was taking flight as the first Black woman to perform the title role in *Firebird* with American Ballet Theatre, another bird was also beginning to soar overseas. That year, Céline Gittens made history as the first Black ballerina in the United Kingdom to dance Odette/Odile, the lead in *Swan Lake*, with the Birmingham Royal Ballet. Being one of few Black or brown ballerinas in a predominantly white company can feel isolating; however, despite our physical distance, simply knowing what Céline and I were accomplishing at the same time gave me a sense of kinship and the fuel to keep fighting for representation both for those who came before and for those yet to come.

Céline was born in Trinidad and grew up in Canada. She began taking ballet at age three with her mother, Janet Gittens, and eventually trained at Vancouver's Goh Ballet Academy. At fifteen, she began choreographing solos for herself for local competitions in Vancouver.

Céline garnered attention for her performance of the Grand Pas Classique variation at the 2006 Prix de Lausanne international competition. That same year she joined the Birmingham Royal Ballet in England and later rose through the ranks of the company to become first artist in 2009, soloist in 2011, first soloist in 2015, and principal in 2016. In addition to her historic turn in *Swan Lake*, she has gone on to dance major roles in popular ballets such as *The Nutcracker*, *Giselle*, and *Firebird*.

At the Birmingham Royal Ballet, her career has continued to flourish under the artistic direction of Carlos Acosta, the famed Cuban ballet dancer who has navigated the ballet world as a brown dancer. While Céline's talents are undeniable, Carlos's presence and leadership, at the highest level, has undoubtedly provided a nurturing environment where she and other dancers can grow as artists. I believe that success is fostered in spaces where a leader is sensitive to the experiences of the student.

Beyond her beautiful performances onstage, Céline is doing incredible work offstage as well. She has a passion for teaching and is playing a huge part in making sure future generations of dancers and artists will benefit from her guidance. She hopes to use over a decade of experience with the Birmingham Royal Ballet to eventually pursue a teaching career.

Although Céline lives and works in the UK, her community in Trinidad remains close to her heart. She is now a patron of Metamorphosis Dance Company based in Trinidad and Tobago, and supports their performances and development. At the time of the announcement, Céline said, "The knowledge that I have gained throughout my pre-professional and professional career is invaluable, and I strongly believe in using my experience to educate and inspire dancers who are passionate about a career in dance."

Passing down history and knowledge from one generation to the next is a tradition deeply rooted in both the Black experience and ballet. I think that today, Black ballerinas hold that same responsibility to hand it down to those who come after us. I see this same belief and commitment in Céline, and her experiences hold unbelievable value and power. I am thrilled that she will be passing that on as a role model and teacher.

"As soon as I could say the word 'ballet,' I knew I wanted to be a dancer."

Alicia Graf Mack

(born 1979)

In 1999, I spent my first summer in New York City attending the American Ballet Theatre (ABT) Summer Intensive program, and saw Alicia Graf Mack for the first time. Her long, elegant body graced posters throughout the New York subway system as the face of Dance Theatre of Harlem's (DTH's) season. I was stunned by her image. Black and brown dancers are often told we are too muscular, our feet are too flat—that we don't have the "ideal" body for ballet. With her long legs and arms, small head, and flexible feet, Alicia undoubtedly *did* have the "ideal" body.

Only a handful of years later, in 2004, DTH had to close their doors due to financial difficulties. I will never forget the confusion and disappointment I felt watching so many Black ballet dancers scramble to find jobs. At the time, I was in ABT's corps de ballet. I remember Alicia, former principal dancer with DTH, whose talents and technique I idolized, asking for an audition with ABT. She was not accepted, not even as a corps de ballet member. While a scarcity of ballet work for Black and brown dancers was nothing new, it was particularly disheartening to see the classically trained professionals of DTH almost uniformly fail to be seriously considered at other predominantly white companies. But Alicia persevered, even though her dance career would now look different from her dreams as a young girl of becoming a ballerina.

Alicia remembers the first time she saw Christina Johnson and Donald Williams perform the pas de deux in *La Bayadère*—how it was the first time she saw a Black ballerina who looked like her. In her senior year of high school, she moved to New York to join DTH, where founder Arthur Mitchell was a mentor and coach. While there, she wowed audiences as the Siren in Balanchine's *Prodigal Son*, as well as in other leading roles.

Although she was forced to cut her ballet career short after DTH was shuttered, Alicia went on to have an illustrious second act, inspiring the next generation as a modern dancer with Alvin Ailey American Dance Theater for nine years. Performing their iconic piece *Revelations* was a particularly defining moment for her.

For perspective, it's an unbelievable achievement for a ballerina who trained her whole life in classical techniques to change genres so suddenly and essentially become a modern dancer overnight. Imagine a pianist switching to the clarinet in order to continue their professional music career—that's what Alicia did, and at the highest level.

Her versatility as a dancer also led to more commercial opportunities, including performances with pop stars Beyoncé, Alicia Keys, John Legend, and André 3000.

While it obviously worked out for the amazingly talented Alicia Graf Mack, this path out of ballet and into other dance genres is all too common for Black and brown ballerinas trying to live out their dreams of dancing professionally.

It has been incredible to watch Alicia on her journey, and also to depend on her as a friend for so many years. She's been an inspiration to me for my entire career and is now giving back as director of the dance division at the Juilliard School—the first person of color and youngest ever to hold that position. The role could not be more deserved, and I couldn't be more proud.

"You transform yourself into a role—you become someone else."

Lorraine **Graves**

(born 1957)

Lorraine Graves is a Dance Theatre of Harlem (DTH) legend. She has acted as Mama, Auntie, mentor, and friend to me and to so many other Black and brown dancers, generations over. I was introduced to Lorraine in 2010 by my friend, my mentor, and former DTH dancer Kellye Saunders, at a critical moment in my professional journey. I remember feeling alone and desperate, dealing with what would become the most severe injury of my career.

This injury began as a stress reaction in my shin while I was on tour in Norfolk, Virginia, Lorraine's hometown. At short notice, she came to my hotel room with a sophisticated ice/compression machine. Though the machine helped ease the pain enough for me to perform the actual steps, it was her emotional support and love that gave me the courage to persevere.

Her guidance would help me get through months of touring, ultimately bringing me to my premiere as the Firebird at the Metropolitan Opera House, a career-changing moment. Only my close circle—including Lorraine—knew the severity of the injury. They rallied around me to ensure I made my historic New York City debut, and their generosity and guidance meant the world to me.

Lorraine began her professional career with DTH in 1978 after graduating early from Indiana University, and she achieved the rare feat of rising to the rank of principal dancer within just one year. Lorraine was surrounded by people of color once she joined the company, and she shared with me that she believed it was that supportive environment that allowed her to reach her potential. So many Black dancers never experience that and, as a result, never fully realize their dance dreams. But her talents afforded her all of these opportunities that she deserved.

Three years after becoming principal dancer, Lorraine became a ballet mistress with the company, helping to run rehearsals and teach. This was in addition to her duties as an active dancer with DTH, proving her maturity and leadership skills even at a young age. These dual roles helped Lorraine find her confidence as a dancer, and, in her words, they gave her "the opportunity to 'see' myself and think about how I *want* to see myself."

Lorraine performed with DTH for seventeen years, making her mark in the company's productions of *Firebird* and *Creole Giselle*, as well as in *Serenade, Agon, Allegro Brillante*, and more. She traveled the world because of ballet, dancing for Princess Diana, Nelson Mandela, Princess Margaret of England, and the king of Norway, among others.

And it's because of Lorraine's extraordinary accomplishments that Black and brown ballerinas today have a road map for knowing that their dreams can be possible.

Lorraine's life, like mine, was completely changed by being a part of ballet. It's a magical thing to be as talented, hardworking, and determined as Lorraine, and the fact that she shared her gifts with me and so many others is something I will always be thankful for.

Francesca Hayward

(born 1992)

Since we are both biracial ballerinas, I immediately felt a connection to Francesca Hayward. Over the years, from afar and with the utmost pride, I've watched Francesca grow into the beautiful artist she is today.

Though we have a decade and a sea between us, each of our journeys have uncannily mirrored the other's. In 2016, Frankie, as her close friends know her, became the first Black principal ballerina at the Royal Ballet in London. The year before, I had become the first Black principal ballerina with American Ballet Theatre.

We eventually met when our paths crossed while performing in international dance galas and festivals. Though there have been very few times in my career when I have shared the stage with other Black principal ballerinas, the opportunities to do so with Frankie throughout the years have always been memorable moments. One that sticks out was in 2018 at the Vail Dance Festival in Colorado. The mountain heights gave me altitude sickness, and Frankie ended up having to replace me in the show. Wearing my costume and performing my role as Juliet, with only a few hours' notice, she showed me love, support, and camaraderie that was everything I could hope for while I was in that compromised state.

Once again following a similar path as Black ballerinas, we starred in two of Hollywood's premier films. In 2018, I portrayed the Ballerina Princess in Disney's *The Nutcracker and the Four Realms*, and in 2019, Frankie starred as Victoria the white cat in the film adaptation of the musical *Cats*. Two Black ballerinas representing ballet in mainstream media is a unique accomplishment that can only move ballet forward and that will hopefully show the next generation what's possible.

Frankie was born in Kenya and raised in England by her grandparents. She discovered her love for ballet at the age of three.

Encouraged by a teacher, Frankie auditioned for a junior division of the Royal Ballet School at age nine and officially entered the school in 2003 at age eleven, and she joined the Royal Ballet company during the 2010–2011 season. Frankie's star continued to rapidly rise as she was promoted to first artist in 2013, soloist in 2014, first soloist in 2015, and then, making history, principal in 2016. Her first major role with the Royal Ballet was as Clara in *The Nutcracker*. She has also danced the lead in *Romeo and Juliet*, *Manon*, *The Sleeping Beauty*, *Coppélia*, and *Swan Lake*, among many other classical ballets.

Frankie has accomplished what few ballet dancers have in this field: she has transcended the ballet world and entered a space where she's being seen beyond the ballet stage. She's in fashion magazines, on late-night talk shows, and in Hollywood films, which is remarkable not just as a dancer but especially as a Black ballerina. Young dancers of color can see themselves in her. It's amazing to experience and witness Black women becoming the face of ballet in real time.

"Dancing was always, from the time I was very young, innate in me. It was something I did as a natural form of expression, and I remember dancing whether anyone was watching or not."

Tai Jimenez

(born 1970)

I came to New York City in 2000 to join American Ballet Theatre (ABT)—naive, ambitious, and hopeful, yet to experience or be educated about the world of ballet and the existence of many Black dancers in ballet history. As the years went on, my eyes slowly began to open. I started to find my voice and take hold of my destiny over at Lincoln Center with ABT, while just uptown, Dance Theatre of Harlem (DTH), the iconic Black ballet company, succumbed to financial hardship. In 2004, DTH closed, and an entire generation of Black dancers at DTH were out of work, many of their careers cut short. This affected me deeply. I remember principal dancers I idolized from the company auditioning for ABT and being rejected from the corps de ballet. It was a devastating time.

And then there was Tai, the *only* DTH member to make a successful transition to a major ballet company. Growing up in Queens, New York, Tai felt a calling to dance early on. During her time as a principal dancer at DTH, she was inspired by the beauty of other dancers, including Virginia Johnson and Christina Johnson, and she performed the title roles of Giselle and the Firebird, as well as several others.

Despite her skills and deep repertoire, Tai found it was a struggle to get work in New York after DTH was forced to go on their hiatus. She was turned down by both major New York–based companies. Though this disappointment led Tai to make history—becoming Boston Ballet's first Black principal ballerina in 2006—it underscores the issue that Black ballerinas have faced for decades: the struggle to find acceptance at prominent classical ballet companies. There was such a huge opportunity to have these talented DTH dancers join the ranks of other major companies, and it is so sad that the potential was not realized.

While DTH, a Black ballet institution, saw its doors shuttered and its dancers scattered, I was eighty-six blocks south, trying to break barriers by becoming the first Black female principal in ABT's history. This was when I started to understand the very real historical crossroads at which I was living as a Black ballerina. I could relate to Tai, and her achievement at Boston Ballet gave me an incredible goal to strive for and a glimmer of hope that it could happen.

Tai eventually turned to other commercial and performing ventures outside of the ballet world. She made her Broadway debut as Ivy Smith in the Broadway musical *On the Town* and also danced with the late pop music star Prince—paving the way for me to do the same years later.

With a passion for choreography and teaching, Tai has transitioned to those areas of the dance world and is continuing to make her mark for the next generation. Tai set an incredible standard that pushed me to dream big! She helped me to see all I'm capable of through the power and importance of representation but also showed the world all we can be as Black ballerinas.

"Dance chose me."

Christina **Johnson**

(born 1963)

Every time I get the opportunity to meet the Black ballerinas who have come before me, it feels as though I'm collecting pieces of my history and myself. I had this feeling meeting Christina Johnson in 2014. She was coaching me on one of the many meaningful roles created for her by Complexions Contemporary Ballet cofounder Dwight Rhoden, a pas de deux called "Ave Maria."

Christina's approach as a coach was very different from anything I'd ever experienced. She generously shared the process she'd used when she'd taken on the role years before, but she took the time to speak with me, to hear me and see me. She wanted to know my thoughts and opinions on the piece and how I wanted to interpret it. I've found this type of investment in dancers within the ballet culture is rare. Coaching can often feel technical and sterile. But having a coach who looked like me and shared similar experiences gave me a different sense of purpose and relationship with the role, something a lot of Black dancers don't often encounter.

For Christina, that sense of belonging was always firmly rooted in dance. When she was a little girl, Christina danced everywhere—around the house, in the garden, in the yard—and she truly believes that dance chose her. When she first started ballet class, she says she immediately felt at home.

After training at the Boston Ballet School, the New York City Ballet's School of American Ballet, and the Dance Theatre of Harlem (DTH) School, Christina began her professional career at seventeen with the Boston Ballet. In 1984 she joined DTH and became a principal dancer within four years. Christina danced with the company for thirteen years, performing leading roles in many ballets, including *Swan Lake, Giselle, Firebird, Prodigal Son*, and *The Four Temperaments*.

Christina was at the peak of her career with DTH when she met Dwight Rhoden and Desmond Richardson backstage after a performance. They let her know they were forming a new company—and wanted her to be a part of it. Ultimately, Christina felt that she was ready for a new challenge, physically and artistically, and made the leap to Complexions Contemporary Ballet.

Founded in 1994, Complexions aimed to mix a variety of styles and methods in a groundbreaking way, with a diverse and inclusive company. It was there that the iconic work "Ave Maria" was created for Christina and Donald Williams, which was the piece that would eventually bring Christina and me together.

Given Christina's passion for inspiring young dancers, it was no surprise that she would go on to teach at renowned companies and schools, including DTH, the Washington Ballet, Joffrey Ballet, Pacific Northwest Ballet, Alvin Ailey American Dance Theater, and Alonzo King LINES Ballet. And it's not just the new generation that's benefited from her influence. During her time on the faculty at Marin Ballet, she taught open adult ballet classes, spreading the joy and beauty of dance to women of all ages, saying that her time teaching at Marin Ballet made her fall in love with the art form even more.

Christina's nurturing spirit has touched countless lives by passing down her knowledge and experience. Because of her, I've gained an understanding of the importance of investing both in oneself and in others. This type of care, coming from a place of love and community, is what moves the art form forward.

"The identicalness of ballet is not that you literally look the same but that you embody the same intention, the same movement. It's another kind of beauty."

Virginia Johnson

(born 1950)

I met Virginia Johnson when she was the founding editor in chief of *Pointe* magazine, one of the most prominent dance publications in the ballet community, and I appeared on its cover in 2002. I had only been dancing for six years and was a newly appointed member of American Ballet Theatre's corps de ballet. Seeing Virginia in a position of leadership in the ballet world at that early stage on my journey gave me a sense of belonging and allowed me to see what was possible. No matter how many times I was told implicitly or explicitly that Black women didn't belong or couldn't be leaders in the ballet community, Virginia was living proof that we did and we could.

It was a monumental time for both me and the magazine. Virginia was a dance icon who'd spent twenty-eight years as *the* principal ballerina with Dance Theatre of Harlem (DTH). But she was also in a position to influence ballet culture on a larger scale as the founder and editor in chief of a premier dance trade publication. It's not often that Black women reach these heights of power in ballet, but when they do, their representation does such an immeasurable service to ballet and its institutions. What's even more incredible is that her publishing roles were only Virginia's second act.

Growing up in Washington, DC, Virginia studied ballet at the Therrell C. Smith School of Dance. Therrell herself had been an aspiring Black ballerina. When she hadn't been able to find schools in segregated DC that would accept her, she studied in New York for five years and eventually moved to Paris. Later Therrell returned to open her own dance school to give other Black dancers the opportunities she had not received. Thanks to Therrell's guidance, Virginia fell in love with ballet and eventually graduated from the Washington School of Ballet. But despite her obvious talent, Virginia heard what so many others like her had: Black dancers had no place in ballet. This fueled Virginia's desire to prove them wrong.

While a student at New York University's dance department in the 1960s, Virginia heard that Arthur Mitchell—who had made history as the first Black principal dancer with New York City Ballet—was creating a new dance company with Karel Shook called Dance Theatre of Harlem. DTH has always represented a commitment to transform the lives of young people in Harlem through art, and to give Black dancers a place in ballet when they were told they couldn't have one. Knowing this was a company where she would be welcomed and could grow, Virginia joined DTH as a founding member. She danced most of DTH's repertoire, with principal roles in performances, including *Swan Lake*, *Concerto Barocco*, *Allegro Brillante*, and *Fall River Legend*. Through works such as *Creole Giselle*, Virginia helped shape DTH's renowned interpretation of classical ballets for generations of ballerinas to come.

After retiring from performing, Virginia took on a different leading role, founding *Pointe* magazine. With a fresh perspective, she energized the coverage of dance by exploring timely topics and highlighting emerging ballet dancers. After her decade-long tenure at *Pointe*, Arthur Mitchell presented Virginia with perhaps the greatest challenge of her career. Trusting her with his vision and knowing her rich history with DTH, Arthur convinced Virginia to accept the role of DTH artistic director. During DTH's hiatus from 2004 to 2012, entire generations of young girls weren't able to see Black and brown ballerinas, but Virginia would be the one to bring the company back. She was also determined to revive the storied classical repertoire that was so uniquely part of DTH's global footprint. Much like what she accomplished as the founding editor of *Pointe*, she introduced DTH audiences to a new generation of ballet dancers. Virginia has long been a mentor to me and a voice of encouragement and leadership. She has led the charge at every stage of her career and continues to prove that success is possible for Black girls and women, both on and off the stage!

Nora Kimball-Mentzos

(born 1957)

For the first ten years of my career, I was the only Black woman at American Ballet Theatre (ABT). It wasn't until the world took notice of my promotion to soloist in 2007 that I even learned about the lineage of Black and brown ballerinas that I was joining at ABT. A legacy pioneered by Nora Kimball-Mentzos.

Until then, I had no idea about Nora's career at ABT, let alone that she was a soloist with the company. Not one person—on the staff, on the board of directors, or even a lifelong fan waiting at the stage door—ever uttered a word to me about her. Yet Nora had set the stage and begun blazing the trail for me decades earlier.

Nora grew up in a family of dancers. After seeing her sister Christina dance with George Faison and Alvin Ailey American Dance Theater, and in the Broadway production of *The Wiz*, Nora developed a passion for dance. At age eleven she began studying at the National Academy of Ballet and Theater Arts in New York City, and eventually trained at the Harkness House for Ballet Arts. The founder, Rebekah Harkness, provided Nora with a scholarship to the school and also paid for her ballet clothing and academic education.

By 1975, while Nora was still a senior in high school, her professional career started to take off, and she received her first professional contract with the Eliot Feld Ballet. And when Germany's Stuttgart Ballet came to New York that same year, Nora felt she was ready to audition. To her surprise, Stuttgart offered her a contract—a testament to her talent and potential. Nora continued to soar overseas, rising to the rank of soloist. After six years with Stuttgart, she joined Netherlands Dance Theater, drawn to their repertoire, which blended modern dance and ballet.

She returned home to the US in the mid-1980s and danced as a soloist with ABT. In addition to her repertoire with the company, Nora performed in the 1987 television production of *David Gordon's Made in U.S.A.* with Mikhail Baryshnikov. She also danced in several Peter Sellars productions, including *The Seven Deadly Sins*, before returning to Europe in the 1990s. In 2018 she danced in Kaija Saariaho's opera *Only the Sound Remains* (also directed by Peter Sellars) at Lincoln Center.

Despite her tremendous body of work and her continuing influence as a performer and teacher, she is often overlooked when Black ballerina icons are discussed. How many others are there in ballet history that we might not be acknowledging?

The historical significance of Nora's career and its virtual absence from discussion gave me a very tangible reason to push to bring our history and contributions as Black women in dance to a wider audience. I hope that sharing even just a portion of her story will result in more of her—and so many others'—contributions being recognized.

"There's nothing like being onstage. Feeling the notes from the orchestra penetrate my soul, and hearing the crowd roar in appreciation, creates the most compelling attraction to this difficult career."

Erica Lall

(born 1998)

In 2012, I met a bright-eyed thirteen-year-old named Erica Lall while in Southern California to speak at one of my home ballet schools, Lauridsen Ballet Centre. Erica came to my talk, and though we met only briefly, that was when our mentorship, friendship, and sisterhood began.

A year later our paths crossed again when Erica joined American Ballet Theatre's (ABT's) Jacqueline Kennedy Onassis School. Once she was with me at ABT, I could walk down the hall of the rehearsal studios and regularly catch her dancing. I knew early on that she was one to watch, and unsurprisingly, she joined the Studio Company in 2014.

Growing up, as with many young dancers of color, Erica saw few professional dancers who looked like her. Over the years she's dealt with racist comments about the color of her skin and her body type, and she's straightened her hair to match the style of her white counterparts. Yet when Erica arrived in New York for the first time, her eyes were opened to new acceptance of her Blackness while she was attending a two-week intensive workshop at Dance Theatre of Harlem: she was finally able to wear tights and pointe shoes that matched her skin tone. This experience gave her a new sense of belonging.

I understand those struggles. I spent the first decade of my career with ABT as the only Black woman, yearning for a sister to share my experience on what is so often a lonely road for Black ballerinas. In 2010 a talented ballerina named Courtney Lavine joined the company while I was a soloist. She was the first Black woman I'd ever been in the company with, and for the first time, I truly felt that I had an ally with a real understanding of my journey.

By the time Erica joined the company several years later, I had already been named a principal dancer, and the environment for Black and brown ballerinas had shifted. There was a real sense of hope for meaningful change and opportunity that hadn't previously existed because there were two other Black women there to support her. I felt a responsibility to give Erica guidance in a way that hadn't been possible before. My hope was that Erica would have a much more definitive blueprint and direction for her career than what Courtney and I had had at the start of ours.

As my friendship and sisterhood with Erica grew, I learned more about Erica's journey. She was raised in Cypress, Texas, her mother is from Jamaica, and her father is from Trinidad. Erica studied tap, jazz, hip-hop, and contemporary dance before joining Houston Ballet's Ben Stevenson Academy when she was nine. She performed with the Houston Ballet in several productions, including seven seasons of *The Nutcracker*, before joining ABT. While at ABT, Erica has performed in *The Sleeping Beauty* and *Swan Lake*, among other ballets.

The combination of a supportive environment and her versatile dance background has given Erica an artistic freedom of expression. Erica has a unique capability and understanding of the importance and value of being able to quickly absorb all that comes with dancing for a premier company like ABT, and of implementing those lessons into her overall approach to her career. She is bold and fearless, and knows what she wants for her life and career. That confidence is something I wish I'd had at her age!

Erica is proof that success is possible when talent has hands-on nurturing and guidance. She is developing into an incredible artist and will be a leading voice for Black ballerinas in the future.

"I went to the ballet barre, and there was something right off the bat that I loved about the music and the way ballet was. It was so beautiful, and it made me feel so special when I was doing it. I just fell in love, and I knew that that was what I was gonna do."

Andrea Long-Naidu

(born 1966)

I first worked with Dance Theatre of Harlem (DTH) in 2010, when a piece was created for me while the company was on hiatus from performing due to financial difficulties. It is also when I first met Andrea Long-Naidu. This opportunity would prove to be a beautiful period in my early career and was the catalyst for great self-discovery. It was the first time I was consistently surrounded by Black and brown dancers in a professional dance environment. While Black skin and exuberant personalities were not hard traits to find at DTH, Andrea possessed both, as well as an incredible energy that shone with confidence. From the moment I laid eyes on her, I just knew this woman had to be a superstar. And after meeting her, I learned about Andrea's impressive journey and what brought her back to DTH as a teacher.

Andrea remembers standing at the barre when she was seven and realizing how much she loved moving to music. She began her dance training with Lupe Serrano at the Pennsylvania Ballet school in Philadelphia—a city rich in Black ballet history, and where so many Black ballerina legends got their start.

At the Dance Theatre of Harlem School, Andrea had a teacher of color for the first time. She has expressed how much it meant to see someone who looked like her, who encouraged and pushed her, despite knowing what obstacles were to come.

Andrea joined the Pennsylvania Ballet as an apprentice for the company before she was accepted into the School of American Ballet (SAB) in New York on a full scholarship. Throughout those two years at SAB, she heard comments about how she might not be the right fit for classical ballet—typically veiled comments that were actually about race.

Andrea was invited to join New York City Ballet (NYCB) in the late 1980s. It was the first time a darker-skinned Black woman danced with the company. As revolutionary as it was, the disparity between how the company nurtured her career as opposed to the careers of her colleagues was eventually too much for her to bear. She made the decision to leave NYCB and joined DTH in 1998. After one year as a soloist, she was promoted to principal dancer and toured internationally, performing principal roles in several ballets.

Drawing on her own experiences, Andrea was inspired to be part of the change in helping historically white institutions be more welcoming toward Black dancers. Knowing how important it was to have a Black ballet teacher at DTH, Andrea also brought attention to the lack of diverse faculty at the major ballet institutions and turned her focus to teaching after she retired from performing in 2008. She has served on the faculty of top companies, such as DTH, SAB, and Central Pennsylvania Youth Ballet. In 2020, Andrea joined the Boston Ballet faculty, where she continues to make an impact.

I have seen firsthand how valuable it is to grow and be nurtured in an environment that celebrates Black and brown skin. Seeing images and footage of Andrea, and so many others, dancing on the stage and teaching in the studio showed me that Black ballerinas can exude strength and beauty in all of our individual glory, without apology. Andrea quickly became, and continues to be, a mentor and sister to me.

"Through dance I have found life. Every new step is like taking a breath of fresh air, a way to discover what it is to be alive."

Ashley Murphy-Wilson

(born 1984)

In 2012, Ashley Murphy-Wilson was at the forefront of Dance Theatre of Harlem's (DTH's) comeback after their eight-year hiatus from performing due to financial difficulties. I attended performances of the new, youthful, and vibrant DTH and got to know Ashley as she was beginning to make a name for herself. An even larger audience was introduced to Ashley in 2014 when she, Ebony Williams, and I had the honor of sharing the cover of *Pointe* magazine, with the headline "Beyond Role Models." Having three Black ballerinas sharing in the celebration of who we are as individuals and what we represented for the future of ballet was such a proud moment for both the dance world and the Black community. The incredible grace in Ashley's spirit was beautifully captured on that cover.

And true to the title of the cover story, Ashley's efforts toward inspiring young people of color have long been a part of her mission. She started dancing when she was three years old in Shreveport, Louisiana. After attending a DTH performance in her hometown and seeing dancers who looked like her for the first time, she knew she wanted to be a ballerina and began her ballet training to become one.

While she was in high school, DTH returned to Shreveport and invited Ashley to participate in a summer intensive in New York. Though she had initially planned to go to college, she chose to accept DTH's invitation to join its junior company, and a year later DTH founder Arthur Mitchell personally invited her into the main company.

Beyond the excitement of starting her professional career, Ashley also appreciated the opportunity to follow her dream in a ballet company that welcomed dancers of color. At DTH new dancers were "adopted" by a family of senior dancers within the company. As an apprentice Ashley was mentored by Andrea Long-Naidu and others, who created a support system that made her transition into a professional career much easier.

Ashley danced for thirteen years with DTH, performing in ballets such as *Firebird*, *Serenade*, *The Four Temperaments*, and *Concerto Barocco*. Upon DTH's return in 2012, she performed many principal roles, including in *Tchaikovsky Pas de Deux* and *Glinka*.

In 2016, looking for a new challenge, Ashley joined the Washington Ballet in Washington, DC. She has performed in *Carmina Burana* and danced roles like the Sugar Plum Fairy in *The Nutcracker*. Offstage, Ashley was featured in the documentary *Black Ballerina*, and she has had the honor of performing for President Barack Obama at the White House.

The lifelong influence of Ashley's DTH family has driven her desire to lead and nurture aspiring ballerinas. She not only danced with the DTH School Ensemble—the performing arm of the school, which continued to operate during the company's hiatus—but also worked with their educational outreach program, Dancing Through Barriers. In addition to these programs, Ashley tirelessly participated in the company's Meet the Ballerina series all around the country, greeting countless youths after her performances and taking the time to answer their questions about life as a ballerina. She believes that our greatest responsibility is to be an example to others, and she continues to prove her commitment to this principle. Ashley has made her mark and is, without a doubt, more than just a role model!

"The ballet was more than the barre. It was more than the plié. It was a lifeline."

Victoria **Rowell**

(born 1959)

Victoria Rowell was the first Black ballerina to ever mentor me—and she set the bar high! I met Victoria while on tour performing *The Nutcracker* with American Ballet Theatre (ABT) at the Kodak Theatre in Hollywood, California. It was 2001, and I was in the very beginning stages of my career, still very much figuring things out. She left a handwritten note for me on the bulletin board that hung at the stage door of the dancers' entrance to the theater, inviting me to her home for dinner. That night I made an amazing discovery: although I was the only Black woman in the company at the time, I was part of a continuing legacy, and her experiences as a Black ballerina mirrored my own.

For Victoria, ballet provided stability and community. She often said ballet was her permanent address—something I could very much relate to at various points in my life. She was raised in foster care for the majority of her childhood, and her foster families encouraged and supported her love of dance, with her second foster mother even teaching her basic ballet steps from magazine illustrations.

When Victoria was eight, she auditioned for a scholarship to the Cambridge School of Ballet in Massachusetts. Though it was supposed to cover just the summer sessions, the founder of the school made sure the scholarship lasted for eight more years.

Victoria went on to earn additional scholarships with the ABT school, the School of American Ballet, and Dance Theatre of Harlem's school. In addition to her time with ABT II, she also performed professionally with Ballet Hispánico and the Twyla Tharp Workshop.

In her twenties, Victoria transitioned from ballet to a career as a model and actress. She is most recognized for her seventeen years playing the role of Drucilla Winters on *The Young and the Restless*, for which she won a Soap Opera Digest Award and numerous NAACP Image Awards, as well as several Daytime Emmy Award nominations. She also appeared on *The Cosby Show* and costarred with Dick Van Dyke in eight seasons of *Diagnosis Murder*.

With a passion for arts education and mentorship, Victoria is a fierce advocate for children. She founded the Rowell Foster Children's Positive Plan, providing structure, support, and encouragement for foster children through the performing arts and athletics. Victoria's love has spread far and wide through her incredible work with foster children, making an impact and setting an example for every child she helps.

Victoria taking me under her wing and treating me like family at that time in my career is a testament to her beautiful heart. She has a tremendous generosity of spirit and an amazing understanding of the power and importance of representation, especially in the ballet space. Our relationship and what it has offered me is a large part of the reason that I am so committed to nurturing the next generation of dancers.

"As long as I can do it physically, I'll do it. Before I lose the joy of dancing, I'll stop and do something altogether different. As for now, there is absolutely no feeling in the world like climbing up on those pickles [pointe shoes]!"

Anne Benna Sims

(birth year unknown)

In 1978, Anne Benna Sims became the first Black ballerina to be a member of American Ballet Theatre (ABT). It's hard to believe that the company was founded in 1939 and didn't see its first Black ballerina for almost forty years! What's even harder to believe is that I didn't hear Anne's name until after I had been promoted to soloist in 2007.

I was extremely disappointed when I could find no documentation of Anne's legacy. In all honesty, I'm still not certain of her rank within the company because of the lack of records, but reports range from her being a soloist to her being a corps member who performed soloist and principal roles. Unfortunately, this lack of accurate record-keeping and acknowledgment is an ongoing challenge in the Black ballet community. I am grateful to and inspired by those committed to uncovering the truth about so many lost legacies.

Unsurprisingly, Anne's story is one of accomplishment and perseverance. She began her dance training when she was ten and was accepted into the trainee program at the Harkness House for Ballet Arts after high school. But despite her talents, she was eventually told that there was not much of a future for Black dancers in ballet and that she was not the right "type" for the main company at Harkness. Determined to follow her dreams, Anne left the country to dance with Les Grands Ballets Canadiens in Montreal, Canada, where she was a member of the corps de ballet.

It was the start of a successful international career. During a break from Les Grands Ballets Canadiens, Anne caught the eye of the director of the Geneva Ballet, Alfonso Cata, who offered her a contract. She accepted, and when he took over the Frankfurt Ballet in Germany, Anne followed, staying for four years and rising to the rank of principal.

In 1977, Anne returned to the USA and joined the Eglevsky Ballet company as a principal dancer. Her versatility finally got her the recognition at home that she had been receiving overseas. After getting rave reviews for her turn in *Ballet on Broadway*—a program of ballets created by Cata and produced by actor Dustin Hoffman—Anne auditioned for ABT and was offered a corps de ballet contract. With that offer, she became the first Black dancer in the company's history. She was in the first cast of the company premiere of Paul Taylor's *Airs*. And when choreographer Antony Tudor cast her in the lead principal role in *Undertow*, people finally began to recognize that Anne could dance a variety of roles in the ABT repertoire.

Though Anne's performances were critically acclaimed, things were not easy for her behind the scenes. An interview with *Jet* magazine in 1981 gives a strong insight into the racism Anne faced. In the interview, Anne recalled an incident where she was told she didn't get a role because she was "too tall." "Let's face it," Anne said, "this tall thing is a euphemism."

Ultimately, Anne's ability to dance in an incredible range of classical works allowed her to perform in top companies all over the world. Her striking and commanding presence and ethereal quality of movement set her apart and caught the eye of so many in the ballet community.

While I came to learn of Anne's career far too late in my own journey at ABT, I am so proud to know that I am continuing on a path she started more than four decades ago. And it has been an honor to witness Black ballerinas come into the company and join me throughout my career, all because of Anne's impact. She fearlessly paved the way, and her legacy deserves to be known and celebrated.

"In the darkness and the futility of the moment you have to get up and keep going, put one foot in front of the other. It's only in trying and keeping going that you achieve. You can't expect that it's all going to happen for you just because you're out there pointing your toes nicely. You have to open your mind and heart, and you must believe in yourself and have faith and hope."

Raven Wilkinson

(1935–2018)

I learned of Raven Wilkinson at a turning point in my life. In 2010, I was at a standstill in my career, struggling to find my voice as a Black dancer and my place as a soloist with American Ballet Theatre (ABT). That's when I came across a documentary on the Ballet Russe de Monte Carlo. I was watching this film about an iconic ballet company, when a Black ballerina came onto the screen and began sharing her story—I was shocked.

Raven Wilkinson was one of the first Black women to dance for a major classical ballet company when she joined the Ballet Russe in 1955. Though she had many career highs and eventually became a soloist, the racism she experienced ultimately forced her to leave the States and move to Europe, where she had more success.

Fifty years later many things remained the same. Like Raven, I was still being told to lighten my skin and "lengthen" my body in order to fit in. Hearing her story helped me realize the ballet world was still holding on to old "traditions" and that I could possibly be the catalyst for the change.

I met Raven in 2011—it was a dream come true. She showed me what true inner strength and perseverance look like. Her love for and belief in ballet always remained, even when the institution of ballet didn't always return that love. Her example gave me the strength to keep pushing for what I wanted out of my career and for the future of all Black ballerinas. Her life was extraordinary, filled with dance, art, adventure, and lifelong friends. Raven loved dance from a young age and remembered being "overwhelmed" when she saw a performance of *Coppélia*. She began ballet lessons at nine and eventually auditioned many times for Ballet Russe director Sergei Denham. Raven later learned that the company was hesitant to hire her, because they often toured the segregated South. But she was determined to keep trying.

In 1955, Raven made history as the first Black ballerina to dance full-time with the Ballet Russe, and she was promoted to soloist in her second season. She became known for the waltz solo in *Les Sylphides* and also performed in *Swan Lake*, *Gaîté Parisienne*, and *Le Beau Danube*, among others.

Yet as her career began to soar, Raven faced constant racism. As the only Black dancer in the company, she had to sneak into white-only hotels while on tour. But at one stop in the South, the hotel manager found out she was Black and asked her to leave. At another stop, she had a life-threatening run-in with the Ku Klux Klan in the middle of a performance. Though her fellow dancers were protective, it all took a toll. Raven eventually left the company and stopped dancing for several years.

Raven's friend Sylvester Campbell, a Black ballet dancer with the Dutch National Ballet, encouraged her to join him in the Netherlands and dance again. She performed with the Dutch National Ballet for seven years before returning to dance with the New York City Opera's ballet ensemble from 1974 until 1985. She then performed as a character actress with the opera company until 2011.

Raven became one of my closest friends and mentors, and one of my fondest memories is of her dancing with my husband at my wedding. She called me before every performance to say, "Let me be the wind at your back while you're dancing." And she always was.

I'll never forget when I was the first Black woman to perform the lead role in *Swan Lake* with ABT at the Metropolitan Opera House and she joined me onstage to present me flowers. When I saw Raven walking toward me from the wings, it hit me that she had never experienced being on that stage taking her own bows. She should have had that opportunity. I dropped to one knee and handed her back the flowers she'd given me—we shared the standing ovation. She, along with every other Black ballerina who'd paved the way for me to be there, had danced through and with me. Raven is my angel, and her wings help me take flight every day and on every stage.

"I discovered that dance wasn't just a fun hobby—it was something I needed to do."

Ebony Williams

(born 1984)

Ebony Williams has always had a strong sense of self and a clear understanding of what beauty and versatility mean to her. She has said, "My role as a Black ballerina is to represent all that's not expected when you see a ballet dancer. Dark, shapely, overly muscular, a funky mover who rocks an Afro." And that pretty much sums up Ebony.

I first learned of Ebony in 2005. She was a bright young star beginning her career with a hot new company, Cedar Lake Contemporary Ballet. She was like no other ballerina I'd ever seen. When she moved her body, it seemed as if it were speaking its own language—a language I didn't completely recognize but innately understood. Her ability to use movement to express herself so vividly is one of her many gifts. But what sets her apart is that she is not defined by one genre. She seamlessly weaves together so many styles that have influenced her.

Ebony and I officially met in 2012 through a mutual friend. After years of admiring her from afar, it felt like I was meeting a long-lost sister. To this day, she's one of my closest friends. We continue to bond as two Black ballerina sisters, sharing our hopes and dreams for our own futures and for the future of dance.

Growing up in Boston, Ebony danced hip-hop with neighborhood friends and picked up dance routines from music videos on television. She first learned tap, jazz, and ballet from a neighbor before enrolling in lessons. Ebony's remarkable abilities earned her a spot in Boston Ballet's Citydance program. Her outstanding skills were recognized, and she was promoted to Boston Ballet School on a full scholarship.

During high school, Ebony took a break from ballet, but she couldn't stay away for long. She ended up attending Boston Conservatory's dance program. There she was reinvigorated as a dancer. After graduation, Ebony became the first Black ballerina to join the Cedar Lake Contemporary Ballet, where she performed for ten years in works by Hofesh Shechter, Crystal Pite, and Alexander Ekman, among others. While at Cedar Lake, Ebony also found incredible commercial dance success. Most notably, she was hired as one of Beyoncé's iconic backup dancers for her "Single Ladies" video—and she has continued to work with Beyoncé on many other videos and tours. Along with the Cedar Lake dance company, Ebony was also featured in the movie *The Adjustment Bureau,* starring Matt Damon and Emily Blunt, and on the television show *So You Think You Can Dance.*

Considering her range of accomplishments, it was no surprise when Ebony was named one of the top twenty-five dancers to watch in *Pointe* magazine. Her immense talent for hip-hop and ballet has given her a beautiful style all her own, inspiring future dancers to know that it's okay to create and take their own path as well.

Ebony continues to empower the whole dance community. She leads youth workshops, with aspirations to leave an enriched legacy—one that increases the acceptance of diverse skin tones and bodies. For Ebony, mentoring and teaching go beyond just the individual dancer. She has said, "The legacy is bigger than just me. It's about our art as a whole." In addition to performing and teaching, she is influencing the dance world through her choreography, working on shows such as *Jagged Little Pill* on Broadway and the movies *In the Heights* and Beyoncé's *Black Is King.* With her extremely diverse career, broad reach, and versatile talents, Ebony has proven herself to be an innovator and role model, challenging ballet norms and influencing the evolution of dance, while proudly and loudly showing us that her Black is beautiful.

Lauren **Anderson**

Delores **Browne**

Janet **Collins**

Stephanie **Dabney**

Michaela **DePrince**

Nikisha **Fogo**

Céline **Gittens**

Alicia **Graf Mack**

Tai **Jimenez**

Nora **Kimball-Mentzos**

Andrea **Long-Naidu**

Ashley **Murphy-Wilson**

Raven **Wilkinson**

Aesha **Ash**

Debra **Austin**

Joan **Myers Brown**

Marion **Cuyjet**

Frances **Taylor Davis**

Robyn **Gardenhire**

Lorraine **Graves**

Francesca **Hayward**

Christina **Johnson**

Virginia **Johnson**

Erica **Lall**

Victoria **Rowell**

Anne **Benna Sims**

Ebony **Williams**

"Coming directly from high school, and having never been away from home, was, I think, the biggest trial I have undertaken. I had to make it on my own without knowing anyone."